SCARLETT JOHANSSON
VS
OPEN AI

The Unknown Facts of The Case Between The Hollywood Star and The AI Tech Giant.

Why Did Open AI Go For Scarlett Johansson?
What's The Detail of The Proposal?
Why Did She Decline?

Ethan Hunter

Copyright © 2024. Ethan Hunter

Table of Contents

Introduction

Chapter 1: Overview of AI and Voice Synthesis Technology

Chapter 2: The Initial Approach

Chapter 3: The Launch of Sky

Chapter 4: Legal and Ethical Concerns

Chapter 5: OpenAI's Response

Chapter 6: Industry and Public Reactions

Chapter 7: AI, Deepfakes, and the Law

Chapter 8: Impact on OpenAI

Chapter 9: The Broader Implications

Conclusion

Introduction

In recent years, the rapid advancement of artificial intelligence (AI) has revolutionized many aspects of our daily lives, including the way we interact with technology. Among the many breakthroughs in AI, voice synthesis technology has emerged as a particularly impactful innovation, allowing machines to generate human-like speech with remarkable accuracy. This technology, however, has also raised significant ethical and legal concerns, particularly regarding the use of individuals' voices without their consent. A high-profile example of these issues came to light in the case between renowned actress Scarlett Johansson and the AI research organization OpenAI.

Background of the Case

The controversy began when OpenAI unveiled a new voice assistant named "Sky" during a live demonstration. Observers were quick to note that Sky's voice bore a striking resemblance to Scarlett Johansson's iconic performance as the voice of the AI operating system in the 2013 film "Her." Johansson, a critically acclaimed actress known for her distinctive voice, had previously been approached by OpenAI CEO Sam Altman with a proposal to license her voice for the new AI assistant. Altman believed that Johansson's voice would help bridge the gap between technology and consumers, making AI more relatable and comforting to users.

Despite Altman's enthusiasm, Johansson declined the offer for personal reasons. Nevertheless, just days before the official launch of Sky, Altman made a last-minute attempt to persuade Johansson to reconsider. When the launch proceeded with a voice that Johansson felt was uncannily similar to her own, she felt betrayed and alarmed. Johansson's response was swift and firm; she hired a legal team and sent two letters to OpenAI demanding transparency about how the voice was developed.

The incident garnered widespread media attention, with many drawing parallels between Sky's voice and Johansson's role in "Her." OpenAI's subsequent decision to halt the use of Sky's voice temporarily only fueled further speculation and debate. Johansson publicly expressed her shock and anger, emphasizing the need for clear legal safeguards to protect individuals' likenesses from unauthorized use in AI technologies.

Chapter 1

Overview of AI and Voice Synthesis Technology

To fully understand the implications of this case, it's essential to grasp the basics of AI and voice synthesis technology. Artificial intelligence encompasses a broad range of computational techniques designed to mimic human intelligence, including learning, reasoning, and problem-solving. Within this field, voice synthesis, also known as text-to-speech (TTS) technology, involves converting written text into spoken words using synthetic voices.

Voice synthesis has evolved dramatically over the past few decades. Early TTS systems relied on concatenative synthesis, which pieced together pre-recorded snippets of human speech. While functional, these systems often produced robotic and unnatural-sounding voices. Advances in machine learning, particularly deep learning, have transformed voice synthesis, enabling the creation of highly realistic and expressive synthetic voices.

Modern TTS systems use neural networks trained on vast datasets of recorded speech. These networks learn to model the nuances of human vocal patterns, including intonation, rhythm, and stress, resulting in synthetic voices that are often indistinguishable from real human speech. One of the cutting-edge techniques in this field is WaveNet, developed by DeepMind, which generates raw audio waveforms from scratch, offering unparalleled naturalness and flexibility.

However, the ability to create lifelike synthetic voices also raises significant ethical and legal challenges. Deepfake technology, which can manipulate audio and video to create hyper-realistic but fake content, has emerged as a major concern. This technology has the potential to impersonate individuals without their consent, leading to issues of privacy, misinformation, and intellectual property infringement.

The case of Scarlett Johansson and OpenAI highlights these challenges in a stark and personal way. As AI technology continues to advance, the need for robust legal frameworks and ethical guidelines becomes increasingly urgent. This case underscores the importance of transparency, consent, and respect for individual rights in the development and deployment of AI systems.

As the story unfolds, it provides a critical opportunity to reflect on how society should navigate the complex terrain of AI innovations while safeguarding the rights and identities of individuals. The outcome of this dispute could set important precedents for the future of AI and its interaction with human creativity and identity.

Chapter 2

The Initial Approach

The roots of the controversy between Scarlett Johansson and OpenAI trace back to a series of interactions between the acclaimed actress and Sam Altman, CEO of OpenAI. These early conversations set the stage for the dramatic developments that would follow, highlighting the complex interplay between technological innovation and personal rights.

Scarlett Johansson's Initial Contact with OpenAI
The initial contact between Scarlett Johansson and OpenAI occurred in September, when Sam Altman reached out to Johansson with an intriguing proposal. Altman, a prominent figure in the tech world, had long admired Johansson's work and saw an opportunity to bridge the gap between technology and human connection through her distinctive voice. The proposal was both bold and innovative, reflecting the cutting-edge ambitions of OpenAI.

Altman envisioned a new generation of AI voice assistants that could offer a more engaging and human-like interaction experience. Central to this vision was the use of voices that users found familiar and comforting. Given Johansson's celebrated voice performance as an

AI operating system in the 2013 film "Her," Altman considered her an ideal candidate for this role. The film had struck a chord with audiences and critics alike, and Johansson's voice was a significant part of its success.

Details of Sam Altman's Proposal

In his proposal, Altman outlined how Johansson's participation could enhance the new ChatGPT voice assistant. He emphasized that her voice could play a pivotal role in easing the public's apprehension about interacting with AI. By lending her voice to the project, Johansson could help humanize the technology and make it more accessible and appealing to a broader audience.

Altman detailed the technical aspects of the project, explaining how her voice would be recorded and processed using advanced AI algorithms to create a highly realistic and interactive synthetic voice. He assured Johansson that the process would be respectful of her time and image, and that she would retain significant control over how her voice was used. The proposal also included a lucrative financial offer, reflecting the high value OpenAI placed on her potential involvement.

Johansson's Reasons for Declining

Despite the appeal of Altman's proposal, Johansson ultimately decided to decline the offer. Her reasons were multifaceted, rooted in both personal considerations and broader concerns about the implications of AI technology.

Firstly, Johansson had personal reservations about becoming the voice of an AI system. While she appreciated the innovative nature of the project, she was wary of the potential for her voice to be used in ways that might not align with her personal values or professional image. The idea of her voice being accessible to millions of users, without her direct involvement or oversight, was unsettling.

Moreover, Johansson was concerned about the broader ethical implications of AI voice technology. As someone deeply involved in the creative industry, she was acutely aware of the rising challenges posed by AI, particularly in relation to deepfakes and the unauthorized use of personal likenesses. The potential for AI-generated voices to be misused, leading to issues of consent and privacy, was a significant factor in her decision.

Johansson also felt a strong sense of responsibility towards her colleagues in the entertainment industry. The industry was already grappling with the impact of AI on jobs and creative rights, as evidenced by the recent strikes demanding better pay and protections against the unauthorized use of AI. By declining Altman's offer, Johansson aimed to take a stand in support of these broader industry concerns.

Lastly, Johansson valued her creative autonomy and the control over her own brand. She had built a distinguished career through carefully chosen roles and projects that reflected her artistic vision. Agreeing to voice an AI assistant, even for a pioneering company like OpenAI, could potentially dilute her carefully curated professional identity.

In her communications with Altman, Johansson expressed her appreciation for the opportunity but made it clear that her decision was final. She articulated her reasons thoughtfully, emphasizing her personal and ethical considerations. Altman, while disappointed, appeared to respect her decision, at least initially.

However, this decision set the stage for the subsequent fallout, as the launch of the Sky voice assistant would reignite these unresolved issues, leading to the legal and ethical battle that followed. Johansson's initial refusal, rooted in personal integrity and industry solidarity, would become a focal point in the ongoing debate about the responsible use of AI technology.

Chapter 3

The Launch of Sky

The controversy surrounding Scarlett Johansson and OpenAI reached a critical point with the launch of the new ChatGPT version featuring an AI voice assistant named "Sky." This chapter jumps into the announcement and demonstration of Sky, the ensuing public reactions, and OpenAI's initial defense of their product.

Announcement and Demonstration of the Sky Voice
OpenAI's announcement of Sky was intended to be a highlight in the unveiling of their latest advancements in AI technology. The company held a live demonstration to showcase the capabilities of the new ChatGPT model, which included a suite of enhanced features such as voice interaction, emotion detection, and even singing. Sky was introduced as a flagship component of this update, embodying the cutting-edge synthesis technology that OpenAI had developed.

The live demonstration featured Sky engaging in conversations with OpenAI employees, displaying a range of responses that were strikingly natural and expressive. The voice of Sky was particularly noteworthy for its clarity, warmth, and emotional depth. During the demo, Sky responded to various prompts with a flirtatious and knowing tone, which immediately caught the audience's attention. This interaction style was reminiscent of the AI voice assistant from the film "Her," drawing immediate comparisons.

OpenAI CEO Sam Altman added to the intrigue by posting the word "Her" on X (formerly Twitter) following the demonstration. This not-so-subtle reference to the film further fueled speculation about the inspiration behind Sky's voice.

Public Reactions and Comparisons to Johansson's Voice in "Her"
The public's reaction to the Sky voice was swift and vocal. Social media platforms, tech blogs, and news outlets buzzed with discussions comparing Sky's voice to Scarlett Johansson's performance in "Her." Many observers noted the uncanny resemblance, pointing out the similar tonal qualities and expressive nuances. The comparisons were so strong that even Johansson's closest friends and fans were convinced that the voice could have been hers.

This widespread perception created a stir, with many questioning whether OpenAI had deliberately modeled Sky's voice after Johansson's. The timing of Altman's reference to "Her" only amplified these suspicions. Fans of the actress and the film expressed both admiration for the technical achievement and concern over the ethical implications of potentially using Johansson's voice without her consent.

Media outlets quickly picked up on the controversy, with headlines highlighting the resemblance and speculating on whether Johansson had been involved in the project. Tech commentators praised the quality of the AI voice synthesis but also raised critical questions about the boundaries of creative and personal rights in the era of advanced AI.

OpenAI's Initial Defense
Faced with mounting scrutiny, OpenAI moved to address the allegations head-on. In statements to the media and on social media platforms, OpenAI executives, including CEO Sam Altman, denied any intentional mimicry of Johansson's voice. Altman asserted that the voice of Sky was not based on Johansson but rather on a different professional actress whose identity they chose to keep private for her protection.

In a detailed blog post, OpenAI explained that Sky's voice was developed through extensive collaboration with voice and screen actors. The company emphasized that all voices used in their products were created ethically and with full consent from the actors involved. OpenAI reiterated that their goal was to advance AI technology in a responsible manner, and they regretted any confusion or distress caused by the launch.

Altman personally apologized to Johansson, acknowledging that the company should have communicated more effectively. He expressed respect for Johansson's decision to decline their initial proposal and stated that OpenAI had paused the use of Sky's voice out of respect for her concerns.

Despite these reassurances, the controversy highlighted significant gaps in the understanding and regulation of AI-generated content. The incident underscored the need for clearer guidelines and legal frameworks to protect individuals' likenesses and creative works in the rapidly evolving landscape of AI technology.

OpenAI's initial defense was a blend of technical clarification and public relations damage control. While they aimed to maintain transparency and accountability, the case opened up broader discussions about ethical AI practices and the responsibilities of tech companies towards artists and the public. The fallout from the Sky launch served as a stark reminder of the complexities and challenges inherent in the integration of AI into everyday life.

Chapter 4

Legal and Ethical Concerns

The dispute between Scarlett Johansson and OpenAI has brought to light numerous legal and ethical concerns surrounding the use of AI, particularly in the realm of voice synthesis. This chapter highlights Johansson's legal action, the correspondence between her legal team and OpenAI, and the broader ethical implications of AI voice mimicry.

Johansson's Legal Action

Upon discovering the launch of OpenAI's Sky voice assistant, Scarlett Johansson was both shocked and incensed by the uncanny similarity between Sky's voice and her own. Feeling that her likeness had been used without her consent, Johansson decided to pursue legal action to protect her personal and professional interests. Her legal team, comprising top intellectual property and entertainment lawyers, moved quickly to address the situation.

Johansson's legal action centered on several key points: the unauthorized use of her voice, potential violation of her right to publicity, and the broader implications for privacy and intellectual property rights in the digital age. Her team argued that OpenAI's actions not only infringed upon her personal rights but also set a dangerous precedent for other public figures and creators.

Letters Sent to OpenAI
In the days following the Sky launch, Johansson's legal team sent two formal letters to OpenAI, demanding transparency and accountability. These letters outlined Johansson's concerns and requested detailed information about the development process of Sky's voice. The first letter emphasized the striking resemblance between Sky's voice and Johansson's, asserting that such a similarity could not be coincidental and raised serious questions about consent and ethical use.

The second letter reiterated these points and pressed OpenAI to disclose the methods and data sources used to create Sky's voice. Johansson's lawyers demanded to know whether any of her previous works, particularly her performance in "Her," had been used as a reference or training material for the AI. They also requested that OpenAI cease the use of Sky's voice immediately and provide assurances that her likeness would not be exploited in the future.

OpenAI responded to these letters by publicly pausing the use of Sky's voice and issuing statements denying any intentional imitation of Johansson's voice. They maintained that Sky's voice was based on a different actress and that the company had followed ethical guidelines in its development process. Despite these assurances, Johansson's legal team continued to seek a more comprehensive response and potential legal remedies.

Broader Ethical Implications of AI Voice Mimicry

The controversy surrounding Johansson and OpenAI has sparked a wider conversation about the ethical implications of AI voice mimicry. As AI technology advances, the ability to create highly realistic synthetic voices raises several critical ethical and legal issues that society must address.

1. Consent and Intellectual Property: One of the most pressing concerns is the issue of consent. Just as Johansson did not consent to the use of her voice likeness, other public figures and private individuals could find their voices replicated without their permission. This raises significant questions about the ownership of one's voice and the legal protections needed to prevent unauthorized use.

2. Privacy and Identity: AI voice technology also has profound implications for privacy and personal identity. The ability to convincingly replicate someone's voice can lead to misuse, such as identity theft, fraud, and the creation of deepfakes. These risks necessitate robust legal frameworks to protect individuals from such violations and to ensure that their identity is safeguarded.

3. Impact on Creative Professions: For actors, singers, and other voice professionals, AI voice synthesis represents both an opportunity and a threat. While the technology can create new job opportunities, it also poses a risk of obsolescence and exploitation. The entertainment industry, already grappling with issues related to AI, must navigate these challenges carefully to ensure fair compensation and protection for creative professionals.

4. Ethical AI Development: The case underscores the importance of ethical considerations in AI development. Companies like OpenAI must balance innovation with responsibility, ensuring that their technologies do not harm individuals or society. Transparent development practices, ethical guidelines, and stakeholder engagement are crucial in building trust and accountability.

5. Regulation and Legislation: The lack of clear regulations governing the use of AI-generated content is a significant gap that needs to be addressed. Johansson's case highlights the urgent need for legislation that defines the boundaries of acceptable use, protects individual rights, and imposes penalties for violations. Such laws would provide a framework within which AI innovation can thrive without infringing on personal and creative freedoms.

The dispute between Scarlett Johansson and OpenAI serves as a pivotal moment in the ongoing dialogue about AI ethics and law. It emphasizes the necessity for robust safeguards to protect individuals from the potential misuse of AI technologies. As society continues to integrate AI into various aspects of life, the lessons learned from this case will be instrumental in shaping a future where technology enhances rather than undermines human dignity and rights.

Chapter 5

OpenAI's Response

In the aftermath of the controversy surrounding Scarlett Johansson and OpenAI's Sky voice assistant, the company faced intense scrutiny and public outcry. This chapter explores how OpenAI responded to the situation, including CEO Sam Altman's statements and public apology, the release of a detailed blog post addressing the Sky voice, and the decision to halt its use.

Altman's Statements and Public Apology

Sam Altman, CEO of OpenAI, took swift action to address the escalating situation. In a series of statements, Altman attempted to clarify OpenAI's position and express regret for any distress caused by the launch of Sky.

Altman denied any intentional imitation of Scarlett Johansson's voice, emphasizing that Sky's voice was based on a different actress. Despite this, he acknowledged the similarities between Sky's voice and Johansson's and recognized the validity of Johansson's concerns.

In a public apology directed towards Johansson, Altman expressed remorse for the oversight and lack of communication surrounding the development of Sky. He admitted that OpenAI should have handled the situation better and announced the decision to pause the use of Sky's voice out of respect for Johansson's objections.

Altman's statements aimed to convey OpenAI's commitment to ethical practices and accountability, while also attempting to repair the relationship with Johansson and mitigate the fallout from the controversy.

OpenAI's Blog Post on the Sky Voice
To provide further clarity on the technical and ethical aspects of the Sky voice, OpenAI released a comprehensive blog post. The post outlined the development process of Sky's voice, detailing the collaboration with professional voice actors and the safeguards implemented to ensure ethical use of the technology.

OpenAI emphasized that Sky's voice was not an imitation of Scarlett Johansson's voice and was created using original recordings from a different actress. The company described its commitment to transparency and ethical AI development, highlighting the importance of obtaining consent from all actors involved in the project.

The blog post also addressed concerns about voice likeness and potential misuse, explaining the technical measures taken to prevent unauthorized replication of individual voices. OpenAI reiterated its dedication to responsible AI development and expressed a willingness to address any further questions or concerns from the public.

The Decision to Halt the Sky Voice
In response to the controversy and ongoing legal inquiries, OpenAI made the decision to temporarily halt the use of Sky's voice. This decision was announced publicly as a measure to address questions about the voice selection process and to give due consideration to Johansson's objections.

By pausing the use of Sky's voice, OpenAI demonstrated a willingness to listen to feedback and make necessary adjustments to its practices. The decision was framed as a gesture of respect towards Johansson and an acknowledgment of the broader ethical implications raised by the situation.

OpenAI's commitment to halting the use of Sky's voice reflected the company's dedication to ethical principles and its willingness to take responsibility for any unintended consequences of its technology.

Conclusively, OpenAI's response to the controversy surrounding the Sky voice involved a combination of public statements, detailed explanations, and concrete actions. The company sought to address concerns, clarify misunderstandings, and reaffirm its commitment to ethical AI development. Ultimately, the decision to halt the use of Sky's voice was a proactive step towards rebuilding trust and ensuring responsible use of AI technology.

Chapter 6

Industry and Public Reactions

The controversy between Scarlett Johansson and OpenAI over the Sky voice assistant sparked a wide range of reactions from various sectors of society. This chapter will shed more light on the responses from the entertainment industry, commentary from AI and legal experts, and public sentiment as reflected in media coverage and social media platforms.

Reactions from the Entertainment Industry

The entertainment industry, particularly actors, voice artists, and filmmakers, responded with a mixture of concern and interest to the Sky voice controversy. Many voiced support for Scarlett Johansson and expressed solidarity with her concerns about the unauthorized use of her voice likeness.

Prominent figures within the industry called attention to the broader implications of AI voice synthesis for creative professionals. Some emphasized the importance of protecting intellectual property rights and ensuring that artists retain control over their likeness and performances.

Trade organizations and unions representing actors and voice artists issued statements condemning the unauthorized use of celebrity voices in AI technologies. They called for greater transparency and accountability from companies like OpenAI to ensure that such practices did not become commonplace in the industry.

Commentary from AI and Legal Experts

AI and legal experts weighed in on the controversy, offering insights into the technical, ethical, and legal dimensions of the issue. Many experts highlighted the challenges of regulating AI-generated content and the need for clear guidelines to govern its use.

Some AI researchers commended OpenAI's technological achievements but raised concerns about the ethical implications of replicating celebrity voices without consent. They called for industry-wide standards to ensure responsible AI development and protect individuals' rights.

Legal scholars analyzed the potential legal ramifications of the Sky voice controversy, including issues related to intellectual property, right to publicity, and privacy rights. They emphasized the need for robust legal frameworks to address emerging challenges posed by AI technologies.

Public Sentiment and Media Coverage

Public sentiment regarding the controversy varied widely, with opinions ranging from outrage to curiosity. Social media platforms buzzed with discussions, memes, and debates about the ethics of AI voice synthesis and the rights of celebrities.

Media coverage of the controversy was extensive, with news outlets, tech blogs, and entertainment websites providing ongoing updates and analysis. Headlines highlighted the clash between technology and celebrity rights, drawing attention to the broader societal implications of the case.

Opinion pieces and editorials offered diverse perspectives on the controversy, reflecting the complexity of the issues at hand. Some commentators criticized OpenAI for its lack of transparency and accountability, while others defended the company's technological innovation while urging greater caution in the future.

In summary, the industry and public reactions to the Sky voice controversy underscored the need for dialogue, regulation, and ethical considerations in the development and deployment of AI technologies. The case served as a catalyst for discussions about the intersection of technology, creativity, and individual rights in the digital age.

Chapter 7

AI, Deepfakes, and the Law

The emergence of advanced AI technologies, including deepfakes, has raised complex legal challenges and prompted calls for updated legislation to address potential harms and abuses. This chapter seems to explore the current legal framework for AI and deepfakes, the need for new legislation, and Scarlett Johansson's advocacy for legal safeguards to protect individuals' rights in the digital age.

Current Legal Framework for AI and Deepfakes

The current legal landscape for AI and deepfakes is characterized by a patchwork of laws and regulations that often struggle to keep pace with technological advancements. In many jurisdictions, existing laws related to intellectual property, privacy, defamation, and fraud are applied to cases involving AI-generated content.

However, these laws were not specifically designed to address the unique challenges posed by AI technologies. As a result, legal interpretations and precedents in this area are still evolving, leading to uncertainty and inconsistency in how courts handle cases involving deepfakes and other AI-generated content.

One of the primary challenges is determining liability and accountability for the creation and dissemination of deepfakes. In cases where deepfakes are used for malicious purposes, such as defamation or harassment, victims may pursue legal action under existing laws related to privacy and defamation. However, proving the origin of a deepfake and identifying the responsible party can be difficult, especially given the ease with which deepfake technology can be accessed and used.

The Need for New Legislation
Given the growing prevalence and sophistication of AI-generated content, there is a pressing need for new legislation specifically tailored to address the challenges posed by deepfakes. Such legislation could encompass a range of issues, including:

1. Consent and Right to Publicity: Laws that require explicit consent for the use of an individual's likeness in AI-generated content, similar to existing laws governing the use of images and recordings in commercial advertising.

2. Disclosure and Transparency: Requirements for platforms and creators to disclose when content has been generated or manipulated using AI technologies, enabling users to make informed decisions about the authenticity of what they see and hear.

3. Accountability and Liability: Clarification of legal liability for the creation, distribution, and use of deepfakes, including potential civil and criminal penalties for malicious actors who produce or disseminate harmful deepfakes.

4. Intellectual Property Rights: Protections for artists, performers, and creators whose work is at risk of being exploited or misrepresented through AI-generated content, including mechanisms for copyright enforcement and licensing.

5. Data Privacy and Security: Safeguards to protect individuals' personal data from being used without their consent in the creation of deepfakes, as well as measures to prevent the unauthorized access or manipulation of sensitive information.

Johansson's Call for Legal Safeguards
Scarlett Johansson's experience with OpenAI's Sky voice assistant has brought renewed attention to the need for legal safeguards to protect individuals' rights in the era of AI and deepfakes. In her public statements, Johansson has called for greater clarity and accountability in how AI technologies are developed and used.

Johansson has advocated for legislation that would ensure transparency, consent, and accountability in the creation and dissemination of AI-generated content. She has emphasized the importance of protecting individuals' likeness, privacy, and intellectual property rights in the face of technological advancements that can easily manipulate and exploit digital representations of people.

By speaking out about her own experience and lending her voice to the broader conversation about AI ethics and law, Johansson has helped elevate the importance of legal safeguards in mitigating the risks associated with deepfakes and other AI-generated content.

In conclusion, the intersection of AI, deepfakes, and the law presents a complex and multifaceted challenge that requires thoughtful consideration and decisive action. The development of new legislation, informed by input from experts, stakeholders, and advocates like Scarlett Johansson, is essential to address the legal and ethical implications of AI technologies and safeguard individuals' rights in the digital age.

Chapter 8

Impact on OpenAI

The controversy surrounding Scarlett Johansson and the Sky voice assistant has had profound effects on OpenAI, ranging from internal turmoil and leadership changes to the company's reputation and future product developments. This chapter delves into these impacts and compares OpenAI's situation with that of competitors like Google's Project Astra.

Internal Turmoil and Leadership Changes
The fallout from the Sky voice controversy has led to internal turmoil within OpenAI, resulting in significant leadership changes and shifts in organizational priorities. CEO Sam Altman's handling of the situation came under scrutiny, with some stakeholders questioning his leadership and communication skills.

As a result of the controversy, OpenAI saw a wave of departures among key personnel, including Ilya Sutskever, a co-founder and chief scientist at the company. Sutskever's departure, along with the disbandment of the superalignment team, signaled a shift in the company's focus away from AI safety efforts and towards other priorities.

The internal turmoil at OpenAI has raised questions about the company's culture, decision-making processes, and long-term strategic direction. It has also prompted introspection among employees and stakeholders about the values and principles that guide the organization.

Effects on OpenAI's Reputation and Future Products
The controversy surrounding the Sky voice assistant has had a significant impact on OpenAI's reputation, tarnishing its image as a leader in ethical AI development. The mishandling of the situation, coupled with allegations of unethical behavior and lack of transparency, has eroded trust among customers, partners, and the broader AI community.

The fallout from the controversy has also raised concerns about the future of OpenAI's products and services. Potential customers may be hesitant to engage with the company, fearing similar controversies or ethical lapses in the future. This could hamper OpenAI's ability to attract new business and secure partnerships with other organizations.

Additionally, the controversy has highlighted the need for OpenAI to reassess its approach to product development and stakeholder engagement. The company must prioritize transparency, accountability, and ethical considerations in all aspects of its operations to rebuild trust and restore its reputation.

Comparisons with Competitors (e.g., Google's Project Astra)

In the wake of the controversy, OpenAI faces increased scrutiny from competitors and industry observers, including comparisons with other companies developing AI-powered products and services. Google's Project Astra, unveiled around the same time as the Sky voice assistant, serves as a notable example.

While both OpenAI's Sky voice assistant and Google's Project Astra offer similar functionalities, the two companies have taken different approaches to addressing ethical concerns and managing public perception. Google's emphasis on privacy, security, and user control contrasts with OpenAI's handling of the Sky voice controversy, potentially giving Google a competitive advantage in the marketplace.

The comparison with Project Astra highlights the importance of ethical considerations and responsible AI development in shaping public perception and market competitiveness. OpenAI must learn from its missteps and adopt a more proactive approach to addressing ethical concerns and building trust with customers and stakeholders.

Summarily, the impact of the Sky voice controversy on OpenAI has been profound, affecting internal dynamics, reputation, and future prospects. The company must navigate these challenges carefully, prioritizing ethical considerations and transparency to regain trust and position itself as a responsible leader in the AI industry.

Chapter 9

The Broader Implications

The controversy involving Scarlett Johansson and OpenAI's Sky voice assistant has raised significant questions about the future of AI voice assistants, the balance between innovation and ethical responsibility, and ensuring that creative rights are protected in this age of AI. This chapter explores these broader implications and their implications for society as a whole.

The Future of AI Voice Assistants
The emergence of AI voice assistants represents a significant technological advancement with the potential to revolutionize how we interact with technology and access information. However, the controversy surrounding the Sky voice assistant underscores the importance of ethical considerations in the development and deployment of such technologies.

Moving forward, the future of AI voice assistants will depend on how companies navigate ethical concerns related to privacy, consent, and the use of personal data. Stakeholders must work collaboratively to establish clear guidelines and standards for the responsible development and use of AI voice assistants, ensuring that they benefit society while minimizing potential harms.

Balancing Innovation with Ethical Responsibility
The controversy surrounding the Sky voice assistant highlights the delicate balance between innovation and ethical responsibility in the development of AI technologies. While technological advancements hold tremendous potential to improve our lives, they also pose ethical challenges that must be addressed thoughtfully and proactively.

Companies like OpenAI must prioritize ethical considerations throughout the entire product development lifecycle, from conception to deployment. This includes conducting thorough risk assessments, obtaining informed consent from stakeholders, and implementing safeguards to protect individuals' rights and privacy.

At the same time, policymakers, regulators, and industry stakeholders must collaborate to establish clear legal frameworks and guidelines that promote innovation while safeguarding against potential abuses of AI technologies. By striking the right balance between innovation and ethical responsibility, we can harness the full potential of AI while minimizing risks to society.

Protecting Creative Rights in the Age of AI

The controversy which involves Scarlett Johansson and the unauthorized use of her likeness in the Sky voice assistant underscores the importance of protecting creative rights in the age of AI. As AI technologies become increasingly sophisticated, there is a growing risk of individuals' images, voices, and creative works being exploited without their consent.

To address this challenge, policymakers and legal experts must explore new approaches to protecting creative rights in the digital age. This may involve updating existing intellectual property laws, developing new regulations specifically tailored to AI-generated content, and empowering individuals with greater control over the use of their likeness and intellectual property.

Furthermore, industry stakeholders must prioritize transparency, consent, and accountability in the development and deployment of AI technologies that involve the use of creative works. By respecting individuals' rights and ensuring fair compensation for their contributions, we can foster a more ethical and equitable digital ecosystem.

In conclusion, this controversy has broader implications for the future of AI voice assistants, the balance between innovation and ethical responsibility, and the protection of creative rights in the age of AI. By addressing these challenges proactively and collaboratively, we can harness the transformative potential of AI while upholding fundamental principles of ethics, privacy, and individual rights.

Conclusion

The case involving Scarlett Johansson and OpenAI's Sky voice assistant has brought to light important ethical, legal, and technological considerations surrounding the development and deployment of AI technologies. As we conclude this examination of the case, let us reflect on its key aspects, outcomes, and implications for the future.

Summary of the Case and its Outcomes
The controversy began with the unveiling of the Sky voice assistant, which bore a striking resemblance to Scarlett Johansson's voice. Johansson, having declined an initial proposal to lend her voice to the project, raised concerns about the unauthorized use of her likeness and the broader implications for creative rights and privacy.

In response to Johansson's objections, OpenAI paused the use of the Sky voice and issued apologies for any distress caused. The company asserted that the voice was not intended to mimic Johansson's and was based on recordings from a different actress. However, the incident sparked wider discussions about the ethical use of AI technologies and the need for clearer legal protections.

Lessons Learned
The case highlights several important lessons for stakeholders in the AI ecosystem. Firstly, it underscores the importance of obtaining explicit consent and respecting individuals' rights when developing AI technologies that involve the use of personal data or creative works. Transparency, accountability, and ethical considerations must be prioritized throughout the entire product development lifecycle.

Secondly, the case underscores the need for clearer legal frameworks and regulations to address the unique challenges posed by AI technologies, including deepfakes and voice synthesis. Policymakers must work collaboratively with industry stakeholders to establish guidelines that balance innovation with ethical responsibility and protect individuals' rights in the digital age.

Future Directions for AI and Legal Protections
Looking ahead, there are several key areas where progress is needed to ensure the responsible development and use of AI technologies. This includes:

1. Enhanced Legal Protections: Policymakers must enact legislation that safeguards individuals' rights and privacy in the face of advancing AI technologies. This may involve updating existing laws, developing new regulations, and establishing clear guidelines for ethical AI development and deployment.

2. Ethical AI Practices: Companies and researchers must prioritize ethical considerations in AI development, including transparency, fairness, and accountability. Responsible AI practices should be integrated into organizational cultures and product development processes to minimize potential harms and ensure societal trust.

3. Collaborative Partnerships: Stakeholders from across sectors must collaborate to address the complex challenges posed by AI technologies. This includes fostering dialogue between technology companies, policymakers, legal experts, and civil society organizations to develop comprehensive solutions that benefit society as a whole.

In conclusion, the case involving Scarlett Johansson and OpenAI's Sky voice assistant serves as a reminder of the ethical, legal, and societal implications of AI technologies. By learning from this case and working together to address its underlying issues, we can build a future where AI serves as a force for good while upholding fundamental principles of ethics, privacy, and human rights.

www.ingramcontent.com/pod-product-compliance
Lightning Source LLC
Chambersburg PA
CBHW050247230526
45470CB00005B/2147